Pasties and Cream

Memories and recipes from a Cornish childhood

Hettie Merrick

truran

ISBN 978 1 85022 197 5

New edition 2005: This reprint 2010
Published by Truran, Goonance, Water Lane, St Agnes, Cornwall TR5 0RA
www.truranbooks.co.uk
Truran is an imprint of Truran Books Ltd

Some of this material was first published by the author in 1984 in 'Pasties & Cream'.
A revised edition was published by Tor Mark in 1998 under the title 'Fed Fitty'.
This edition incorporates all the original material with considerable additions of
both text and photographs.

Printed and bound in Cornwall by R Booth Ltd,
The Praze, Penryn, Cornwall TR10 8AA

Cover artwork: www.theantiqueimage.com
Cover design: www.alixwood.co.uk

Title page photograph: Hettie Merrick's mother and father
at St Peterstide Feast in 1933. Hettie is in her mother's arms
and her brother John in his father's;
Aunt Violet and Uncle George are in the background (HM)

INTRODUCTION

Long ago Porthleven was just a coastal hamlet with an inlet between two ridges through which at high tide the sea rolled meeting a stream which flowed down Methleigh Valley, known locally as 'the bottoms'. The little cluster of houses situated in the middle of Mount's Bay faced the full might of the Atlantic Ocean and was named after a little known saint, St Elvan, one of whose toes is preserved in an enormous glass case in mid-France. This saint lived about two miles inland where a small rural area is still called St Elvan. Nearby were two other saints' abodes, Breage to the west and Sithney to the north, where the church for Porthleven stood, a long walk for the villagers Sunday worship. It is said that funerals could be very lively affairs as the bearers needed to stop at stiles on the way for rests and refreshments.

The local men eked out a living farming and fishing like their neighbours at the end of a shingle beach which stretched from the hamlet two or three miles along the coast to Gunwalloe Fishing Cove. About two hundred years ago

'locals proudly boasted that you could walk from one side of the harbour to the other on the moored boats without getting your feet wet' (RCM)

surrounding land and mine owners decided that it could be profitable to build a harbour at Porthleven which would enable them to import coal and timber needed for their estates and to export china clay recently discovered on Tregonning Hill by William Cookworthy in 1746. At that time their trade depended on supplies overland to and from Gweek, a busy tidal creek on the Helford river. Though Gweek was not a great distance away it was a wearisome and slow journey for horses pulling heavily laden carts up and down the hills to deliver goods.

A great project was undertaken beginning with a fine long pier which acted as a breakwater and helped form a large outer harbour. Two quays were then built, one from each side of the inlet, leaving a gap in the middle to form a harbour entrance which could be secured by baulks in storm force gales providing shelter in a deep inner harbour. It was an ambitious project that never fully repaid its investors, but all this work brought in skilled stone masons, carpenters and builders. It was soon a thriving port; new money bought larger fishing boats and the locals proudly boasted that you could walk from one side of the harbour to the other (a long stretch) on the moored boats without getting your feet wet.

Cornish food is economical, plain and wholesome, with a few special treats. No matter that modern diets are low in carbohydrates, yeast and saffron cake, pasties, splits, heavy cake and cream are as well loved as ever.

'It's a food that'd stick by 'ee,' is a remark often heard. Cornish mothers heave a sigh of relief when their sons marry local girls. They know they'll be 'fed fitty' and at least be sure of the weekly pasty.

The recipes I've gathered for this book form the background to the main traditional meals – breakfast, dinner, tea and supper that were eaten by most families during my childhood at Porthleven in West Cornwall during the 1930s and 1940s. Many have been handed down to me by members of my own family; others are from people who have become well known locally for their own particular speciality. I hope many people will be tempted to make their own pasties and try some of the enduring Cornish favourites.

Mother took in visitors, the name for paying guests in Cornwall. As my bedroom would be needed I would be off to stay with Gran Gilbert or Aunt Hettie in the country. My favourite hideout there was the earth closet. It was just a few yards from Aunt's front door and surdily built of stone on the side of the house, the path to it leading onto an orchard of apple trees and one lonely medlar.

The door was solid and not rotted along the bottom so was safe from small creatures, mice etc; inside it was high and roomy. A long painted wooden seat with two holes with lids went along the whole length of the back wall. In one corner of the seat were matches and a candle in the battered enamel holder and 'paper', in the other corner a box of Jeyes powder.

It was a good place to daydream especially if it was raining and I would sit for ever on one of the lidded seats. In front of me high up was a row of twelve inch windows through which I could see branches of trees waving to and fro. Two panes were broken and a rambling rose had found its way through together with ivy which clung to the wall. Up there leaves were caught in dusty cobwebs and often there would be a spider hanging from the ceiling on a single fine thread.

Sitting there I would light piece after piece of paper watching them slowly burn; they would blacken and curl, and when let go they floated gently to the floor. This 'paper' was not the the *West Briton* cut up into neat squares and threaded with string that we had in both my grandparents 'loos'; but whole pages of brightly coloured gardening catalogues. These were not as interesting as trying to match squares of the *West Briton* to find the end of sentences abruptly cut off. I was always called to 'come in'.

Uncle Fred was a keen gardener who ordered catalogues and studied them diligently.These arrived by post with rare visis from the postman who had a bumpy journey by bicycle down the long lane to the house. He was always welcome and would prop his cycle against the wall by the back door and come in for a cup of tea and a piece of white (yeast) cake. sitting in Uncle's comfortable armchair. Aunt would catch up with all the local news.

Life seemed all comfort to me at *Content* ; even going to bed was a delight with my bed welcomingly warm. Aunt had wrapped a hot 'sheath' (shelf) from the oven of the slab in newspaper and placed it in my bed while I said my prayers.

BREAKFAST

The start of the day was usually a rush, but at home we managed porridge or shredded wheat followed by bread, toasted through the bars of the Cornish range on the prongs of a long wire toasting fork. Mother bought Dundee marmalade, sold in white, shiny pots. My grandparents on both sides considered all this new-fangled. They ate bread, butter and golden syrup, which we called treacle, or jam, or saffron buns with cocoa.

Food, though, has never tasted so good as it did at *Content*, an isolated farm cottage (now swallowed up by RNAS Culdrose) where I spent many of my childhood holidays with Aunt Hettie and Uncle Fred. First thing every morning eggs were fetched from a long row of chicken houses. I was allowed to carry my own egg for breakfast, warm and smooth in my hand. One old fowl was a household pet. She was lame and no one had the heart to kill her, so I had 'Miss Clutterbut's egg' for breakfast, or so I was told.

My aunt made bread once a week, putting the loaves into round cake tins to bake. To cut slices, she would hold the loaf crooked in her left arm resting against her pinny and cut the bread towards herself with a worn but razor-sharp knife. As the week went by the bread got drier and the slices thinner, till by bake day the slices were like wafers. The bread was eaten to the last crust and rarely thrown out for the chickens. They got a good mix of vegetable peelings boiled up outside in an iron pot placed on a triangular brandis over a good wood fire.

BREAD

Plain flour must always be used for yeast cookery and strong flour gives the best results. Fresh yeast is easily obtainable in Cornwall, but dried yeast is almost as good. The main thing is to keep the yeast dough out of any draughts. A sunny spot is good, but room heat is sufficient now that cold kitchens are a thing of the past.

Fifty years ago bowls of dough were put to rise in the rack of the Cornish range – 'the slab'. My aunts sponged their yeast by making a hole in the flour, pouring the yeast in with a little milk and sugar, sprinkling some flour over to cover. The bowl would be covered with a damp cloth and put in the rack. Every now and then the corner of the cloth would be lifted and they would peep inside to see if the yeast had bubbled through. When it had, they lifted down the bowl, mixed the dough, pummelled it and then put it back again to prove, or 'to plumb', as we say.

Croust at *Content*. Uncle Fred with the Lugg family (HM)

It all takes time. There is an expression still used when someone does something they might regret: 'She'll wish her cake dough' said with a shake of the head.

Bread Recipe

Note: The quantities are for more than one loaf as it is a waste of oven space to bake just one. Bread freezes well.
1½kg/3lb strong white flour
25g/1oz yeast and 1 tsp sugar creamed together
50g/2oz lard
3 teaspoons salt
900ml/1½pt tepid water (or three quarters water, one quarter milk)

Whisk the yeast and sugar into half the liquid. Put the flour and salt in a bowl and rub in the fat. Pour in the yeast and the remaining liquid. Mix and knead well till the mixture leaves the bowl clean. Cover with a cloth or put into a lightly greased polythene bag to prove. When the dough has doubled in size, knead it again and mould into loaves. Put into greased tins to just below the top. Prove again till the bread is above the tin. Put in a hot oven 425°F/220°C/gas mark 7 and bake for one hour. Turn out of the tin at once, onto a cooling rack.

Bread sops (Gran's between meals filler)

Cut a thick piece of stale bread from a loaf, break it up into small pieces and place in a cup. Pour on boiling water and drain it off, squeezing the bread with the back of a spoon till the bread is dry and crumbly. Season with salt and pepper. Place a large piece of butter on top and eat at once with a teaspoon. It is impossible to make this with modern sliced bread: home made bread or bread that will crumb is the only kind suitable. It was sometimes made with cocoa.

THE VILLAGE

Porthleven was, in a way, divided in three. Downlong or downtown meant the harbour, the Gue, a steep lane and the Unity, a street named after a long abandoned mine; up-long or up-n-town included the coastguard station, Peverell Terrace and the oldest inhabited area, Gravesend with its cottages perched perilously along the cliff's edge. In this area drowned mariners were buried with no ceremony or depth until a Helston solicitor protested to

Bowden's
Boatyard,
Porthleven
1930s (RCM)

parliament and succeeded in getting the Grylls' Act passed in 1808 ensuring decent Christian burial in churchyards for all drowned sailors.

Beyond Gravesend the road leads to High Burrow or Ibra, as locals say, where there are traces of ancient mine workings. The coastal footpath is hard-going in places due to coastal erosion but leads to the Bar and the Loe, believed locally to mean pool. The bar of shingle, exactly halfway between Porthleven and Gunwalloe Fishing Cove was formed many years ago by the silting up of the shingle beach preventing the river Cober which flows through neighbouring Helston reaching the sea. A walk from Helston or Porthleven around this large tranquil pool situated in the beautiful Penrose estate is a great experience, but the pool is dangerous. We children were warned never to put a foot into its waters in case we drowned; we were scared enough for once to do as we were told. Across the bar the footpath leads to Fishing Cove where Porthleven men occasionally visited to help seine fish or cut withies (tamarisk), the supple branches of this tree-like shrub needed by fishermen to make their crab pots.

On the western side of the port, Breageside, known as Little Nation and shadowed by the hilly mound of Chapel Downs seemed almost foreign to us facing them across the water of the outer harbour. The stream flowing down the valley had at one time divided the parishes of Breage and Sithney, a division that was still vaguely felt in my childhood. Had Breagesiders once been a law unto themselves? It was not so long ago that Breage wreckers were in fierce conflict with Sithneyside wreckers over 'wreck', the local word for flotsam and jetsam, an important part of the local economy missed in these days of modern shipping. There were many fights over the dividing line. The close-knit community of Breage may have accounted for a saying commonly said to this day from Land's End to the Lizard 'you're like a stranger from Breage' when you meet someone you haven't seen for a while.

Along the top road the houses are tucked into a menacing high rock face, but across the road on the brow of the hill there is an almost hidden seat overlooking the harbour. Past the houses the road leads to a footpath that passes an ancient wrestling field and leads on to disused tin mines along the coast. Men walked miles to work deep down in these mines whose workings went far out under the seabed, the minestacks tall and proud still stand defying time and weather.

On the lower road at Breageside there are a few houses and a quaint old pub, the Ship Inn; no one seems to know its age. Nearby in 1863 a lifeboat the *Agar Robartes* later replaced by *Dash*, was installed in a stone-built house. Although there were a few successful rescues it was soon realized that gale force winds proved the lifeboat too difficult to launch and it became obsolete in 1929 the year I was born. I can remember there was sadness when people talked of 'losing' their lifeboat. Along the harbourside new stores were put up, one so high that its roof was higher than the top road of Breageside sixty feet or more above. There were doors in the wall under this roof through which clay was tipped; down below on the quayside of the building, it was shovelled out and loaded on to cargo boats for export to where? I never knew.

On this side of the harbour most of the fish was landed and Pawlyn's had good business as buyer and merchant. Here a dark strange cave is next to a round lime kiln where an aunt told me she used to cook small crabs in the heat of its wall.

At the head of the harbour on 'the Bank' two large wooden sheds dominated the area. They were built on long posts and rickety steps led to the top floored in part where boat plans were laid out. Underneath, shipwrights made sturdy boats. Porthleven had such a good name for craftsmanship that even yachts were commissioned. Launch days were special and everyone turned out to see them especially when a yacht commissioned by Lord de la Warr, the *Lady Hilda* slid down the slipway in 1909. Behind the sheds, across a road, the

11

harbourmaster's office was built between a high wall which encompassed a large timber yard. In an alcove in the wall of the office a large barometer was placed behind thick glass. It was forever called 'the Glass' and the fishermen visited it every day.

Near the timber yard over a stream were Kitto's net works, where heavy, enormous looms produced drift nets which got dipped in creosote and were then laid out to dry on the moors near the withy field. I liked its pungent smell as it wafted up to us on our way to school. Just off the corner of the Bank was an important area called 'the Square'. The Square, a sort of crossroad, was a meeting place where there would always be about half a dozen men standing to discuss catches, the weather or latest news (few people owned a wireless, even fewer a telephone or car). Nearby stood 'the Gate'; this substantial wood gate guarded a coal yard and was never opened but was, and still is, used as the village notice board. Grandfather, who lived a stone's throw away, went down first thing every morning to scrutinize it. If anything important, a death or funeral date pinned up he would return immediately to inform Gran before going over to check the Glass. On his way he would pass a smithy full of long handled tools and a furnace which glowed a brilliant red.

It was a magical place with its jolly blacksmith banging his hammer or shoeing a horse. The blacksmith, a popular reciter, nicknamed Freddy Pudding, would occasionally call in at Gran's on his way home from work and recite her favourite ode 'For People Will Talk'.

Here in the heart of the village a couple of cobbler's shops were popular places for the men to meet for a chat or singsong. A few yards away a chemist shop had a steady but quiet trade as Porthleven's legendary doctor, Dr Elliston, a large boisterous man, dispensed his prescriptions on the spot taking down this or that large green, blue or brown bottle from a high shelf and measure liquids out by eye straight into his own named medicine bottle; a new cork was pressed tightly into its neck and holding the cork and bottle in one hand he shook the contents violently. Dr Elliston blamed many of his patients' ailments on their Cornish fare and his greatest wish was to ban pastry from the face of the earth.

I think families paid one shilling a week to be 'on the panel' for 'free' treatment. His surgery, a cold outhouse a few yards from his home, had a narrow passage leading to his consulting room where we sat facing each other, our knees almost touching, wheezing and sneezing, waiting for his bellow 'NEXT'. It is true to say that he was worshipped by his patients, but he scared me to death.

Uncle Fred and Aunt Hettie outside the front porch at *Content* (HM)

DINNER TIME

After breakfast at *Content*, water was fetched from the spring below the henhouse. The water gushed out freezing cold from a pipe into a granite trough, spilling out and running down the valley. Water was carried to the house in large brown earthenware pitchers, but first we filled up the split bicycle tyres for the chickens to drink from.

When it was time to cook dinner (which was usually eaten at noon), we went up to the garden to get the vegetables, and to pick fruit for tarts for 'afters', or for tea. Beef and pork were eaten for the main daily meals: though my mother often cooked lamb with mint or caper sauce, I cannot remember Gran cooking it. Gran liked a piece of beef with a bit of fat. She bought a little frying steak surprisingly often, and streaky pork for the under-roast.

Rabbit in season was very popular; we got ours from *Content*, where Uncle Fred used snares (thankfully banned now) or one that had been shot in the harvest field fleeing from the last standing corn. Some men went lamping with dogs or used ferrets to chase rabbits from their holes. The downs nearby were a network of warrens.

Beyond the Downs, across the Bar Gran and Granddad Bray lived at Gunwalloe. They lived well: there was a daily bowl of cream from Sam, Granddad's brother next door, who kept two Jersey cows. Gran also made cream from the milk she fetched in a large jug twice a day from her neighbour's farm. There was so much cream that Gran – 'Mother Matt' as everyone in the village called her – made all her own butter. Granddad kept pigs and chickens, so they had plenty of eggs and pork. Vegetables and corn for his hens came from the local farms in exchange for the odd day's work by Granddad. Apples and medlars came from Hingey Orchard, gooseberries and rhubarb from the garden. Granddad was very fond of honey: this he had to buy! It was wartime and every Saturday Gran came over to us with a basket full of eggs, butter, cream, and a fruit or seed cake. She and Aunt Hettie bought dried fruit by post from southern Ireland during rationing: a purchase of which my father strongly disapproved.

Granddad Bray ate only under-roast potatoes (see page 23) with his meat and vegetables. I never saw him eat fish, but he did like lobster. One day while wrecking with Father after a storm, they saw a stranded lobster high and dry on some rocks. Granddad got to it first and claimed it, much to Father's annoyance! When wrecking you would put any 'find' above the tide line while you continued your search; this automatically acknowledged your 'right' to it and this right was always honoured by everyone.

Puddings were limited to a choice of three – junket, milk puddings, or fruit tart, always with lashings of cream and accompanied by a single cracker biscuit. The tarts, when cooked and sugared, were carefully put onto a second plate to protect the cloth from juice; they waited on the table, the wafer-thin top floating on a sea of warm juicy fruit. At *Content*, Uncle Fred had a dinner-plate-sized tart for himself. Aunt Hettie's would be a medium plate and mine a large tea-plate. I felt it was like the three bears sitting at table.

One day Thelma, my eldest cousin, brought her fiancé Charles over to *Content* for the day. He was considered a bit posh. He worked at 'the Mount' as under butler for Lord St Levan. When his tart was put in front of him he was very puzzled. I don't know if he managed to eat most of it, but Aunt Hettie always chuckled as she remembered his face when he realised he was expected to eat it all.

In winter broth was made often, simmering on the top of the range all morning. Sometimes large white beans, which had been soaked, were added. But for many people, of course, the best dinner in Cornwall is the famous pasty:

Matthew, Mark, Luke and John
Ate a pasty five foot long.
Ate it once, ate it twice,
Oh my Lor', it's full of mice.

All Cornish children learn this ditty and have their own pasty from toddler days, and any visitor to a Cornish town at noon cannot fail to notice a cross-section of people, smart office men and women, hefty workmen, youngsters and mums pushing prams, eating their lunch as they go along, 'a pasty in their hand,' as a local song puts it. So the traditional pasty must be the first item in any section of a Cornish recipe book.

Pasty Pastry

500g/1lb strong white flour (pinch of salt optional)
125g/4½oz margarine Echo
125g/4½oz lard
200ml/7fl oz water to mix

Put the margarine in the freezer for ten minutes. Place the flour in a bowl and rub in the lard. Grate the margarine and stir into the flour with a knife. Pour in cold water. Mix with a knife till absorbed. Knead the mixture a little and leave it at least half an hour before using – or make it the day before and store in the fridge overnight.

Filling for one Cornish pasty

50g/2oz finely sliced swede (always referred to as 'turnip' in Cornwall)
25g/1oz finely sliced onion
75–100g/3–4oz beef (skirt or chuck)
175g/6oz sliced old potatoes
salt and pepper

Keep the sliced potatoes in a basin of cold water till needed. Trim off any gristle and cut the meat into 6mm/¼in pieces including some fat. Cut off 150g/5oz of the pastry and shape it roughly like a ball. Roll out into a 20cm/8in round. Place the onion along the centre of the pastry and cover with a layer of turnip. Sprinkle with pepper and a shake of salt. Place the meat along the top and to the ends. (The 'ends' are the corners and the cook must make sure that the meat is spread into the corners.) Season the meat with a little salt. Top this layer with most of the potato, salt lightly and place the remainder of the potato on top. Seasoning is important to the taste of a pasty and only experience can perfect it.

Moisten the further half of the edge of the circle with water and fold the other half over to seal. Press the sides of pastry together, from the middle outwards towards each end, pressing gently and firmly. 'Crimp' the edge from right to left by folding the pastry edge over and over in a rope pattern, tucking in the end when you reach the other side. Place the pasties apart on a flat baking tray. Brush with beaten egg or milk.

Some people put a knob of butter in the pasty. I don't think this is necessary, but it may be traditional. There was often very little beef available and in that case the

16

butter would help make gravy. Pasties are 'pressure cooked', I don't make a hole in mine to let the steam out, though some people do. Place in a hot oven 425°F/220°C/gas mark 7 on a shelf three quarters of the way up from the bottom and 'bake like fate' for 15–20 minutes. Check the pasties: if nicely brown, place them on a lower shelf and turn the oven down to 350°F/180°C/gas mark 4 and cook for a further 25 minutes, then turn the oven off altogether. Keep the oven door shut and leave for a further 10 minutes. Remove from the oven and let them rest for a few minutes before serving.

Many pasty variations can be found in the *Pasty Book* which I wrote for Tor Mark.

Mock flaky pastry for sausage rolls, etc

Roll out 450g/1lb made-up pastry into an oblong. Dab 125g/4½oz butter on two thirds of the area. Fold over the unbuttered side and fold over again. Rest the pastry for 30 minutes. Roll out and fold in three again. Rest a little before use. (If you use frozen pastry, defrost, roll out, and fold in three again. Rest 15 minutes before using.)

Broth, for 4 persons

900ml/1½pt stock or water
450g/1lb flank or stewing beef, in one piece
a quarter to a half cauliflower head
3 large slices of swede
2 onions or shallots
half a leek,
2 or 3 carrots and a parsnip sliced
salt and pepper
parsley
bay leaf

Fry the meat on all sides for a minute in a little butter. Add the water or stock, bring to the boil and simmer for one hour, skimming off any scum. Add the all the vegetables chopped into bite-sized pieces, except the cauliflower. Simmer for another 30 minutes. Add the cauliflower cut into large pieces, the seasoning, bay leaf and parsley. Simmer till cooked. Remove bay leaf and parsley. Check the liquid level and remove the meat to a plate. Cut up the meat and return to the broth if you wish, or reserve it to eat with boiled potatoes. There should be nearly two litres of soup; add dumplings if liked.

Rabbit Pie

Skin and clean the rabbit and wash again in salted water. Disjoint and place the rabbit pieces in a saucepan with a little carrot, onion, swede, salt, pepper and a bay leaf. Cover with water, bring to the boil and simmer until tender. Place pieces of rabbit in a pie dish with pieces of turnip and carrot: remove the bay leaf. Pour some of the liquid into the dish. Cover with thick pastry, placing an upturned eggcup in the dish to keep the pastry up in the middle. Bake in a hot oven 450°F/230°C/gas mark 8 till the pastry is cooked. Chicken or fowl pie can be made in the same way and parsley can be added.

Beef and Tatie Pie

for 4 persons
450g/1lb stewing beef
1 large onion
half a small swede
500g/1lb 2oz potatoes pepper and salt
125g/4oz made up pastry
1 or 2 cups water (approx. 250 to 500 ml)/½–1pt

Cut the beef into small chunks and fry a little, with a knob of butter. Place in a saucepan with one cup of water, onion and seasoning. Cover with a lid, bring to the boil and simmer for at least 30 minutes. Add the swede and potatoes sliced up thickly and simmer till the vegetables are almost cooked. (If the stew dries out add water to make some gravy.) Season and pour all the contents into a deep pie dish. Cover with rolled out fairly thick pastry, trying not to stretch it and immediately place in an oven at 450°F/230°C/gas mark 8 to cook for 15–20 minutes. Serve with cabbage or other vegetables.

Stew

for 4 persons
600g/1lb 5oz stewing steak
8 potatoes
1 medium swede
4 or 5 carrots and parsnip if liked
2 or 3 onions, shallots or leeks to taste

Cut the meat into small chunks and fry in a large saucepan with a knob of butter until brown on all sides. Cover the meat with water. Bring to the boil, then simmer for 45 minutes. Add the chopped, prepared vegetables, pepper and salt. My aunt used to say, 'Give it a good gallop', but simmering is what is required, stirring it around occasionally and adjusting the liquid with water. Dumplings can be added ten minutes before dishing up.

Dumplings

Mix 50g/2oz shredded suet to 100g/4oz self-raising flour and a good pinch of salt. Add about 75ml/3fl oz water to make a soft dough. Divide into eight shapes and poach on top of the stew for ten minutes.

Many years ago, my newly married sister-in-law made my brother stew once a week. One day he hinted he wouldn't mind a dumpling or two. Sylvia asked my mother for instructions. Mother said, 'You double the amount of flour to suet and simply mix it all with water.' Sylvia did this, using the whole packet of suet. The lid of the saucepan rose higher and higher, when they came to eating their meal, the meat and vegetables had disappeared entirely; but love prevailed and my brother ate most of it.

Leeky Pie

(Mrs Sylvia Oliver, Goon Rinsey)
Cut 500g/1lb chuck or braising steak into cubes and season with a little salt. Barely cover with water and casserole it till tender. Meanwhile, partly cook some leeks, then cut them up and layer them on top of the meat. Spread cream over if you have it handy (you can tell this recipe came from a farm!) or butter and pepper well, cover with flaky or pasty pastry and bake till brown.

In the village just up from the Square a small post office did business in someone's front room. Opposite was Mr. Blight's store. This store could have strayed straight from an American cowboy movie. You entered by granite steps up from the road and immediately smelled paraffin. A few steps and you were beside a wide, long mahogany counter that went three quarters of the way down the room. Behind the counter the whole wall was covered with drawers of all sizes also in rich highly polished mahogany; in them were dried fruits, lentils, sugar, etc. Flour was sold in white cotton sacks which Gran washed, unpicked the stitching and saved to make handkerchiefs showing me how to hem and do drawn-thread work. In the far corner streaky, middle and gammon bacon hung from huge hooks and you chose which you wanted and the thickness it should be cut.

I often went with Gran to the store where she sat on a chair while being served. I was fascinated watching Mr Blight package sugar, peas or whatever; he would swipe a piece of blue or brown strong paper from a large roll, trim it with a knife to size and place the paper on one side of a magnificent brass scales and put a weight on the other, open the necessary drawer and scoop out almost exactly the right amount of goods and tip it on the paper in a heap. When weighed he placed it on the counter, deftly put two sides together then folded the paper over with a couple of neat pleats, turned in one side, upended the package tapping the contents down and tucked in the remaining paper tight and firm. Not a grain of sugar or a currant could escape.

Both Mr and Mrs Blight were very, very, plump. Across the counter his white aproned middle looked monstrous to my eyes which were level with his apron strings tied in a bow across his middle. Gran told me that they had been very good to the fishermen in hard times. Mr and Mrs Bright were great musicians and put on musicals like *The Pirates of Penzance* with local singers in my father's youth. I always felt that the whole shop should have been preserved as a museum, but sadly it was not.

Just off the Square towards the sea a few more shops looked out over a small L-shaped quay where nets were mended and older men sat on a low bench sheltered by a high wall. On the other side of the wall a longer quay was home to a giant crane which was higher than the Commercial, a new inn nearby. The customs' house was here and a high two storied cellar which at one time stored salt for curing pilchards bound for Spain and Italy.

There were four stores in the village where fish was cured; the largest just off the Bank was a big square building, with iron steps outside zigzagging up to second and third floors. So much fish was exported that there was a rhyme which I think began: 'God bless the king of Spain, long may he reign'.

Along this Customs' Quay coal boats unloaded. There was an air of excitement when a boat was due; sometimes it had to lay off at sea till tide and conditions were right. We children were pleased when we came out of school to see the docking space empty and kept our eyes open for a sign of the pilot boat going out; when it did we watched at first high up on the Terrace, a bird's eye view of the whole harbour. It was a skilled and difficult job guiding a large boat in but space had already been made, the fishing boats moved safely out of the way. As the boat neared the Gap we dashed down steep Army Hill by the Big Ben like town clock and rushed to see it edge through with barely an inch to spare.

Once in harbour the boat slowly turned and was nursed to the quayside. Immediately huge heavy chains which had been unwound from big granite bollards went rattling down the harbour wall. We children were constantly sent packing. It seemed to take hours this mooring, but once secured the crane came into use swinging deep 6ft round iron buckets into the holds where men shovelled coal furiously into them. They were inched back slowly, heavy and ominous. It was noisy and hazardous handling them to tip their load. Almost at once sturdy little horses pulling deep sided carts were trotting to and fro carrying coal to the waiting empty coal yards. Everywhere was covered in coal dust making your nose itch.

Sometimes a timber boat arrived unloading at Breageside but it was never as exciting.

'the crane came into use swinging deep 6ft round iron buckets into the holds where men shovelled coal furiously into them' (RCM)

VEGETABLES

Fishermen have no time to dig a garden. When in from the sea there is work to be done, nets to be mended, and the boats seen to. Their houses, anyway, were built either perched on the edge of the cliff or sheltering underneath, close to the road, with little ground either front or back. There might just have been enough room to grow a bay tree for the pilchards, or a bush of boy's love, useful to keep the flies away. Potatoes and swede, bolstered with carrot, leek, onion, parsnip and broccoli cauliflower grown by the farmer were the vegetables eaten, helped out with dried peas and lentils.

Granddad Gilbert with peaked cap and old fishermen friends
From left to right: Pascoe, Bowden the Butter-man, Jack Pearce, Gilbert (Jack False), John Thomas (Harbinger John), (Willie) Kitchen shoemaker's father, Jack Strike. (HM)

My father never tasted a tomato till he got married and never got to like them. Celery, lettuce or cress he considered rabbit food. Mother was in her element cooking. She would cook strange things at home, like mushrooms or artichokes, and made delicious sauces. Father couldn't abide sauces and, like most Cornishmen, hated food 'mucked up'. For him potatoes were served very plainly: boiled with fish, under-roast every other meal, chips or raw tatie fry for tea. Under-roast was the easiest. The slab was always lit and potatoes in the oven left the top clear for a kettle on the boil, the iron, cooking vegetables or the large oval iron pot for washing clothes.

Under-roast Potatoes

Bring peeled potatoes to the boil, cook a little and drain. Grease a pie dish with butter or dripping and fill with potatoes. Add a couple of small onions and a few pieces of swede if liked. Season with salt and a good shake of pepper. Brush some dripping over the potatoes or cover with a few bacon rinds, and half fill the dish with hot water. Place another dish over the top as a lid, or cover with greaseproof paper. Put in a hot oven for a good half-hour. Take off the paper and cook for another hour or so until the tops of the potatoes are nice and brown and the water almost gone. The result should be crispy brown topped potatoes with mushy bottoms. Sometimes a piece of meat would be cooked in the middle and always Granny Gilbert baked a roll of pastry across the top.

Raw Tatie Fry

Fry two rashers of streaky or other bacon in a frying pan. Add sliced raw peeled potatoes till the pan is nearly full, sprinkle with some salt and pepper and pour in water until the potato is almost covered. Cover pan, bring to the boil and cook gently for about an hour. (Some people add onion.) The water should be absorbed, but not dried out.

Gran Gilbert, who lived at the bottom of the steps linking the Terrace with the centre of the village, 'up long' with 'down long', was the pivot round which all her grandchildren gathered She could always produce something for us to eat and often warmed us up on winter evenings with raw tatie fry, bread or cocoa sops (see page 8) or a cup of broth (see page 17).

Potato Cake

Mix together
450g/1lb mashed potatoes
100g/4oz sultanas
two tablespoons each self-raising and plain flour,
50g/2oz chopped suet or butter
salt to taste.

Shape into rounds and bake till brown and crisp.

Mashed Swede

Prepare a swede and cut into pieces. Put into a saucepan and cover with cold
water. Add some salt, bring to the boil, and cook until tender. Drain off the water.
Season with a good shake of pepper and a little ground nutmeg, and add more salt
if need be. Keep hot and, just before dishing up, mash well with a good tablespoon
of thick cream or butter.

This was Mother Matt's recipe. I remember watching the colour of the mashed
turnip change dramatically when the cream was added. It tastes wonderful but
I can never bring myself to be so extravagant.

On summer evenings retired fishermen sat, perhaps on their favourite seat, at
the foot of Salt Cellar Hill facing the pier and open sea. On their left were two
or three shops and a few cottages. A row of Victorian bay windowed houses
built high above the road curves towards the Town Clock and the Men's
Bickford Smith Institute founded by the family of that name at Trevarno. I
think this institute may have been a reading room, common in villages where
men gathered to hear news read out, probably from the *West Briton*. In the
1800s few people could read or write and it was not till the 1840s that 'the first
grant to education allocated less money for the entire country than had been
spent on Windsor Castle stables.' About 1870 an Act stated that children
must be literate and numerate before they could leave school.

Grandfather, born in 1865 always grumbled about 'that dratted Act', but did
write with a fine copperplate-like hand. I do not know how old he was when
he left school, but he was shipwrecked at 13 years of age on the Longships.
News of the loss of the fishing boat reached Porthleven quickly with no word

of the crew, who, in fact, were safe and walking home from Penzance. When the crew rounded the wall towards the Square the women were weeping and wiping their eyes with their black aprons fearing them all lost.

On summer evenings the setting sun steals slowly in putting the town clock in shadow but lights up Bay View Terrace in a golden glow which reflects in the water below and gradually sweeps around to the Seat at the foot of Salt Cellar Hill. When I was a child I must have been 'minded' by Granddad as I remember playing marbles there, making a circle in the dusty road, sometimes with cousin Marjorie and school mate Dulcie Treloar whose Grandfather always sat next to mine. I was quite jealous as her Granddad wore a gold ring in one ear and mine did not. Some summer evenings the band practised in a room a short distance away. We explored all around and a favourite excursion was to go into a passageway of the old fish cellar just up from the Seat. It was forbidden territory, but if we saw the heavy door open we crept inside.

A few steps in the passage turned sharp left and immediately we were in total darkness, pitch black. All along on our right the wall was littered with heaps of old netting, coils of rope, oars, boxes, boots and lines and stank accordingly. We carried on feeling our way till we saw a glimmer of light appear and then full daylight. Before us was a big open space which framed an old rusting winch; we leaned on it and looked out. Before us was a perfect picture. People were walking by far below and we could see the Gap and derrick on the far quay and further on the Ship Inn and Breageside. It seemed worth the risk of being told off if discovered.

AFTERS

Britain is famous for its puddings and the Cornish share a great love of afters. We ate jam roly poly, egg custard, tarts made with blackberry, blackcurrant, gooseberry, apple, rhubarb or plum; also prunes and custard or prunes still warm with clotted cream – delicious. Rice, sago and tapioca were often made as well, and mother always made treacle pudding on Sundays. Jellies, blancmange and Russian cream were usually reserved for Sunday tea, along with trifle. There is a tale that one Porthleven man ate jelly every morning for breakfast. This idea of him wobbling to work everyday struck mother as funny. Her sense of humour carried her through her busy days.

Clotted Cream (home made)
Pour at least four pints of fresh milk into a large saucepan. Let it rest all morning and carefully place the saucepan on the stove. Bring it slowly to a temperature just below boiling; it must not begin to rise. Gently put it to one side and leave overnight in a cool place. Next morning skim off the top into a dish. Use the remaining 'scalded' milk for puddings or milky drinks. Real Cornish cream is made by scalding the cream from separated milk until a delicious thick crust is formed.

Bread Pudding
Crusts or half a stale loaf soaked in a litre of water
a couple of handfuls of currants and sultanas
stale cake or buns, if you have them, crumbled
grated rind and the juice of half a lemon
a little mixed peel
a pinch of salt
2 tablespoons sugar
a few chopped dates
125g/4½oz margarine
2 tablespoons syrup
1 or 2 eggs
1 teaspoon bicarbonate of soda
1–2 teaspoons mixed spice

Squeeze the water out of the bread and place the bread in a bowl. Add all the other ingredients except the margarine, syrup, lemon juice and bicarbonate of soda. Melt the margarine and syrup in a pan and add to the mixture. Mix the bicarbonate of soda with lemon juice and stir in immediately; mix all together. Smooth out into a large greased baking dish and fork a pattern on top. Cook in a slow to moderate oven: around 325–350°F/170–180°C/gas mark 3–4 for about an hour or more. Sprinkle with a little sugar and eat either hot or cold.

Cooked Apple

We ate apple all ways. Simply stewed and eaten with custard, or stewed with suet dumplings on top; large apples would be cored and filled with brown sugar, baked and brought out of the oven at just the moment when the fluffy apples were lifting the scored skin around their sides and the juice like toffee in the tray; baked with a coat of pastry they looked even bigger. There were tarts of course, and apples cooked with a topping of sponge or baked in the oven sliced between thin slices of bread and butter, cinnamon and sugar.

Autumn was a feast in those days. Most of us knew or had someone in the family working on a farm and were given a bag or two full of windfalls. Nowadays orchards and fields are being cleared to make way for housing or larger fields and those wonderful old-fashioned apples are disappearing; some gone for ever.

Mother Matt's Apple Tart

Pile an old dinner plate or pie dish with as much peeled and sliced cooking apple as it can hold. Moisten with a tablespoon of water. Cover the apple with pastry, rolled out quite thinly, making sure you don't pull the pastry too tightly, so that it can shrink a bit. Bake in a hot oven till cooked. Remove from the oven and carefully lift off the pasty pastry top slice around the edge with a knife before lifting. Sugar the contents and when the apple has cooled a bit replace the lid. Serve slightly warm with plenty of cream.

Shortcrust pastry is not suitable for this tart. Pasty pastry holds together better.

Ample Amber

This is the one pudding which was unknown to mother. Our evacuee's family brought it down and it was soon a great favourite.

Line a sandwich tin with shortcrust pastry; sprinkle it with some bread pieces or baking beans and bake blind. Meanwhile, cook prepared 450g/1lb or so cooking apples in a very little water add sugar to taste when cooked.

Separate the yolks of 2 eggs and whisk yolk with a good pinch of mixed spice into the hot apple. Put aside to cool a little. Whisk the whites till stiff and gradually fold in four tablespoons sugar to make meringue. Remove beans or bread from pastry case and fill with apple mixture. Top up with meringue and put in slow oven 300°F/150°C/gas mark 2 till the top is nice golden colour. Eat hot or cold.

Junket

Warm one pint of milk to blood heat with two dessertspoons of sugar. Pour two teaspoons of rennet into a large jug and add the warmed milk and sugar. Pour out at once into two or three dishes, which you should have placed where they need not be moved till dinner time. Do not put in the fridge. When needed, sprinkle with nutmeg to taste, and serve with at least 25g/1oz cream per person. Junket can be made an hour or more in advance. Rennet is a bit difficult to find these days. Vegetarian rennet is not as acceptable to the Cornish taste. Real rennet can be obtained from Langdales Ltd, Chase Road, Northern Way, Bury St Edmunds, Suffolk, IP32 6NT.

Rice Pudding with Egg

Make rice pudding in the usual way. Ten minutes before dishing up, add one or two beaten eggs to the pudding, stirring it in carefully so that the skin is not disturbed. Sprinkle the pudding lightly with nutmeg. This was a favourite with Granny Gilbert, who made wonderful rice puddings. She could not afford cream, but nursed the pudding along all morning on the bottom shelf of the oven, adding extra milk now and then. She would often add an egg for extra goodness.

Russian Cream

2 eggs
600ml/1pt milk
25g/1oz gelatine
50g sugar

Add gelatine to enough hot water to melt it. Separate the egg yolks from the whites into two separate bowls and beat the yolks with the sugar. Put the milk on to boil and when the milk begins to rise in the pan stir in the beaten egg yolks and sugar. Remove from the heat. Stir in the gelatine. Beat the egg whites till stiff enough to turn the bowl upside down without them slipping out! Whisk the egg yolk mixture onto the egg whites and pour it all into a serving dish. Put in a cool place to set. Russian cream is usually made the day before you need it, and is nice served with seedless grapes. I am always puzzled as to where this much loved delicate sweet came from, as it is so different from all other Cornish cooking.

Fishing being the industry of Porthleven many young men and women worked in one of the four net factories. With the onset of World War 11 there was a great demand for camouflage nets. The mesh needed for these was too large for the local looms and soon almost every kitchen had a hook beside the Cornish range to make them by hand. When the net was halfway across the room it was gathered and draped up with a bit of orange binder twine and you continued in this way till the net was complete. The nets were enormous. Piles of netting and balls of twine littered the place. Even mother, who was not local, learned how to hold the scantle and tie knots with a good speed. We children had to wind the twine onto the wooden needles every evening before we went to bed. A wooden box of them had to be full of these for morning, so that the adults could work much quicker next day. Pap was very happy and busy delivering twine to all his family besides making his own nets. Everyone felt it was their duty to contribute to the war effort. The village had never been busier and it was a welcome increase in income.

South-westerly gales are ferocious and in Mount's Bay waves roll in with unbridled force. Aunt Violet and Uncle George lived in one of the tiny houses at Gravesend in the 1920s and one terrifying night fled with their three small children to grandparents in comparative safety across the road. To Kathleen, the eldest, the clearest memory of that night was that they broke most of Gran's shinny balls (Christmas baubles) which they discovered in the bedroom. This cottage survives to this day and defiantly withstood the tremendous storm in 1979 when Porthleven's harbour was ravaged by a hurricane storm causing immense damage. Great granite quoins were torn out of the outer harbour and the inner one battered, the water gushing over the protecting baulks causing boats to float level with the road.

The village looked like a battlefield but no lives were lost, everyone fully aware of the danger of high heavy waves and the need to keep clear of all roads around the harbour. As in all fishing villages there have been tragedies too painful to relate; they are hidden in the corner of every local person's heart and often remembered with great feeling and respect.

Porthleven is surrounded by saints – Breaca, Sezny, Elvan, Corin and Guenole, so it is not surprising that religion held an important place in the life of the community. A new Church of England was built in the village in 1839 partly funded by the local squire at Penrose. Sithney or Breage was a long way to walk even for the pious. The new church was not attended by the local fishing families who were more taken with the teachings of Wesley and had already since the 1790s, begun meeting in a long room where the town clock now stands. Soon this room became too small and it was proposed that a larger room be built at Gravesend where most of the fishermen lived.

Mr Martin Matthews, former curator at Helston Museum, told me that the guarantor insisted that this building have a chimney as he was doubtful that this new religion would last and it was important to ensure that the building could then be used for something useful! But this building soon became overcrowded and after using a few more places, Peverell Road, the Fishermen's Chapel was built in 1863.

Mr Matthews says the money for this was raised by the fishermen who agreed to set aside a bag of fish from every catch to be sold to fund it. As in most Cornish villages there was soon dissent on how things should be run and so a group of worshippers formed a breakaway group and decided to build their own chapel. In 1883 a fine Wesleyan Chapel was erected further down just off the main road, its grand cathedral-like front inspiring an unnamed wit to make up a catchy ditty:

They built the church upon my word as fine as any abbey,
and then they thought to cheat The Lord, and built the back part shabby.

I remember local preachers with affection, particularly Mr Geach, a tall wrangly man with a voice that reached every corner of the chapel. He loved using long words like 'procrastination', 'tribulation', and 'confrontation' for which most of us waited with bated breath to hear. But a favourite was Mr Simon Rule who was as short as the other long; he chose favourite hymns and told us amusing moral stories. Mr Rule was a net/sail maker who worked in Stodden Cowls' loft just yards from my grandparents' home and I often sat in its doorway as he and two other men sat cross-legged on the floor, sails stretched out flat as far as I could see, stitching away with long steel needles pushing the thread through with the help of a leather and metal glove. Mr

Rule took his concert party by char-a-banc to distant villages, the trips an event themselves especially once when the laden vehicle broke down in the middle of nowhere. A catastrophe in those days.

Sundays meant worship three times a day for most Porthleven residents. If you went nowhere, you could be called 'hathens'! Our chapel (Peverell Road) was very homely and revivalist. Prayer meetings were held monthly after evening service. Mr Pentecost, the organist, departed and all the people upstairs came down below to sit in the body of the chapel in a close, cosy gathering.

Anyone, it was usually one of the men, could get up and say a prayer or give a testimony which would be encouraged by someone's 'Hallelujah' or 'Praise the Lord', one of the ladies might pitch in with 'Blessed Assurance' or some other well liked hymn. In summer these meetings were transferred to the quayside at Salt Cellar Hill where just hymns were sung in the open air. Grandfather strongly disapproved of Church (C of E) with all that 'bowing and scraping' saying he bowed to no one but his Maker. He did not like statues or robes but would put up his hand to his cap if he met Revd Gotto, a well liked priest who was ecumenically minded before any of us had ever heard of the word, but was never invited to join in any chapel services till very late in his ministry.

The village was home for a brief spell to a small group of members of the Salvation Army, but strangely this religious expression did not catch on, perhaps it was the uniform, but Army Hill remains to their memory. The Christadelphians came and stayed and have a small but strong church, as have the Apostolics.

FISH

Fish was always abundant and cooked simply, either fried or boiled. No sauces were needed to disguise the flavour of fresh fish. Grandfather, a retired fisherman, was well looked after by the younger men. When the boats were due in, he'd go down long for a 'turn' returning with a a few fish hooked in his fingers or laced through the gills with a piece of string. He and Gran Gilbert kept a bussa in the back kitchen. This was a huge stone jar for salting down fish. We ate ling, whiting, pollock, mackerel, pilchard, megrim, ray, sometimes cod, but never conger eel.

Our evacuee George, once caught a huge conger eel with hook and line off the pier, my brother John hauling a smaller one in soon after. They proudly took their catch home to Mother who refused point blank to cook it, so they went down to Grandfather who said 'Thraw 'n back'. George was dumbfounded so they want over to Pawlyn's, the fish merchant, who paid them 7/6d for the two. I think they treated themselves to fish and chips once or twice.

Occasionally we ate John Dory, a big spiky fish with a lovely taste. At my grandparents, Pap would cook the fish. Fresh mackerel poached in salt water

Group of retired fishermen – boatyard in background (HM)

33

with butter slowly melting over, boiled potatoes and mustard, is a feast in itself. Sometimes if the fire was low enough in the grate, he would 'scrowl' them. The mackerel would be split open and the middle bone taken out, salt and pepper shaken on and the fish laid on a griddle across the fire. He cooked steak this way also and the fire would spit and flare. The taste was unforgettable.

If the weather was very good, the mackerel would be cleaned, boned, peppered and hung out to dry in the sun. The popular fish dish in Porthleven was marinated pilchards; Gran always had some on the go. Also a great favourite was dried salt cod; it was known as niffling. The fishermen often followed the fish up the Irish coast, crossing Britain through the Caledonian Canal, and would work down the east coast before returning home. On one such trip Granddad, aged 24 was the eldest on board. The skipper, John Toy, his future brother-in-law was 19. The *Louis*, a 40ft mackerel driver belonged to John's great uncle and had been built for sail of wood 'on the bank' at Porthleven by local shipwrights.

They were days of necessity. The young men were very experienced; Granddad and I expect others went to sea at an early age, but perhaps only fishermen can fully appreciate the confidence and trust of the great uncle, too ill to go to sea himself – and the responsibility of the young man to take the precious boat so far from home. No one in the village would take a boat to sea on a Sunday. Sunday was for worship. Pap met Grandmother when he was berthed at Falmouth and she caught his eye in chapel.

THE GUNWALLOE RECIPES

To my surprise one day, Mrs Dale, a farmer's wife, asked me if I had ever seen a booklet printed in 1939, written by members of the Methodist Chapel at Gunwalloe. It's a little treasure, full of worthy advice, sayings, and best of all their favourite recipes some of which follow.

Toffee Pudding for Children

(Mrs Hocking, Truro)
225g/8oz golden syrup
115g/4oz butter
115g/4oz brown sugar
3 slices bread 125mm/½in thick

Place the syrup, butter and sugar in a frying pan and stir till melted. Remove crusts from bread and cut into two inch squares. Soak these in milk and fry them in the toffee for about 5 minutes. Place in a hot dish, pour on the remaining toffee and serve with cream, I expect.

Fig Pudding

(Mrs Debra Jenkin, Nanspean Farm, Gunwalloe)
115g/4oz shredded suet
115g/4oz flour
115g/4oz breadcrumbs
115g/4oz brown sugar
340g/12oz figs [or dates]
1 large apple
1 teaspoon baking powder
150ml/5fl oz milk

Chop the figs and apple fine, mix flour and baking powder well, add dry ingredients with milk to moisten them. Pour into greased basin and steam for 2½hours. (Sufficient for 8–10 persons.)

Banana Pudding

(Mrs HC Lugg, Post Office, Gunwalloe)
225g/8oz self-raising flour
115g/4oz butter
115g/4oz caster sugar
4 bananas
2 eggs

Beat all together before adding flour. Bake about 1½hours.
300–350°F/150–180°C/gas mark 3–4. This is an interesting recipe which results
in a thick pancake-type pudding which is nice hot or cold. Try half mixture and
bake in an 20cm/8in greased sandwich tin for 45 mins.

'Helston Pudding'

(Miss Margaret Freeman, Tregadjack, Mawgan)
115g/4oz raisins
115g/4oz currants
115g/4oz flour
115g/4oz ground rice
115g/4oz sugar
small piece of peel
115g/4oz breadcrumbs
175g/6oz suet
1 teaspoon mixed spice
a little salt
some milk
1 teaspoon bicarbonate of soda

Clean the fruit, cut the peel finely, and dissolve the bicarbonate of soda in the
milk. Mix together all the dry ingredients and add the milk. When thoroughly
mixed, pour into a well greased basin, cover with greased paper and a floured
pudding cloth tied securely. Stand in a saucepan full of boiling water and boil for
two hours.

TEA

Everyday teatime in our family was a brief meal – cup of tea and a bun or perhaps a piece of bread, butter and syrup. I often went to Aunt Violet's for tea. She had a large family and I squeezed in beside my cousins on the wooden form around the table, drinking strong dark cocoa and eating coconut haystacks or a piece of 'jam paste' – which I liked so much it became their nickname for me. Sometimes Uncle George would make his speciality, potato fritters. What a wonderful way to fill up a growing family. A few potatoes would be sliced very finely, dipped into fresh batter and dropped into hot fat in the frying pan. They were usually cooked in the scullery beside the kitchen and brought to us in relays. We could hear them sizzling, and then they would come in, all hot, crisp and salty.

Gran sat on a hard chair at the back of the room, her hands resting on the crook of her walking stick, Aunt Violet sat by the slab with a short cane handy by to keep order. Her two older boys often got a crack. They were two 'lembs' (limbs of the devil). Tucked away in the corner there always seemed to be a new baby which Aunt Violet rocked and sang off to sleep in a sweet, soft voice.

All the bakers sold good bread. Mother bought most of her bread from Johns, one of whose sons brought bread around in a large wicker basket to the customers' houses. He often sat down for a short spell, resting his arms at the end of the table, probably while mother was hunting for her purse. His transport was a pony and a neat little van. The milkmen too delivered milk from their ponies and traps, carrying large cans of milk, and measured out the pints into jugs at the doorstep. Mr Curnow, our main supplier, often waited for a few minutes. Mother, who worked at a hectic pace usually needed to wash up a jug. Visitors, family and Miss Cox all had to be looked after.

Miss Cox, was an aristocratic permanent guest with her own two rooms. She had bread and milk at 7pm promptly every evening. Bread at just the right degree of staleness was sliced about ⅛ inch thick, trimmed of crust and then cut into tiny squares and placed in a broth bowl. Half of pint of milk with a pinch of salt was heated to boiling point, poured into the bowl and taken at once to her living room.

We children often had bread and milk also, but it was roughly torn up or cut into one inch dice with the crust on. We preferred this as Miss Cox's seemed so insipid, but we thought in unfair all the same, as we were told it was sinful to waste crust because of the people starving in China. Miss Cox was very religious and we felt she should have eaten crusts as well. Once brother John and George, the evacuee hid under her table and almost frightened her to death.

With good fresh bread, there is nothing to beat a slice of 'thunder and lightning'. Cut a thick slice of fresh bread and spread the surface well with golden syrup and then thickly with clotted cream. Some people dribble a trickle of syrup over the top to make a pattern. The cool cream, sweet syrup and crusty bread make a wonderful combination. Cream on splits, sprinkled with sugar is also popular. Gran Gilbert, who had a sweet tooth often made sandwiches with Turkish Delight, fruit cake, ginger biscuits, banana, jam, grated chocolate or Mars bars.

For special occasions, a few iced fancies, slab cake, Scribona swiss roll, or congress tarts would be bought. Wearne's, who baked in Helston and rented a little shop on the quay had a good selection and they would be bought for chapel teas.

Electricity arrived in the early part of the last century. It took several years for grandfather to consent have the 'lectric put in. I sympathised with him a little as I liked all the ceremony of fetching the lamp, polishing the glass, the trimming of the wick and Pap lighting it with a paper spill from a little pile he made and kept on the side of the slab, the Cornish range. However, the family were worried that the house might catch on fire so he gave in at last, but insisted that it should only be installed in their living room. This was fine; I could still go to bed carrying a candle in its blue enamel holder, read for a short while then blow out the flame. I loved watching the smoke curl upwards as the fiery wick slowly died. The family had done their best but everyone had a chuckle including Pap, when the first quarter's bill arrived for the sum of sixpence.

Looking back they all sound strong, capable and vigorous and one can only wonder at their energy and independence of mind. They could sound a dour lot but they had fun as well as work. Any newlyweds could expect a din outside their window for most of their wedding night. On Christmas Eve people met up at midnight carrying lanterns (there were no street lights) and

**Grandma Harriet and Granddad Jack Gilbert
– my father's parents about 1920 (HM)**

sang carols all round town till dawn. They probably sang Thomas Merritt's new carols and knew all the words by heart.

Hallowe'en was also celebrated when small groups of people would go around disguised. If they knocked on your door you were obliged to provide cocoa and perhaps heavy or saffron cake. Evidently Gran was very annoyed when her five sisters-in-law 'took her in' one Hallowe'en. Gran was from Mylor and had arrived after her marriage in a fine pony-drawn wagonette.

There were socials and concerts in the Sunday school in winter, carolaires on the Square, an exciting regatta in the harbour on Lifeboat Day and the yearly carnival in summer. The men had successful football and cricket teams and the Men's institute where they played snooker all year. Women were unwelcome in this hallowed den.

I often slept at grandparents Gilbert and went to school from their home. One day John, minutes late for school burst into my classroom arms waving shouting 'we've got a baby sister!'

Neither of us had an inkling of this unexpected event, though we suspected that babies came from ladies' tummies; it was a mystery how it happened or how they got out! Mother's figure had been well disguised with her cotton sleeveless wrap around, a shapeless garment worn by almost all housewives at that time.

Joyce born at the onset of war, was a model baby who slept well and was as good as gold, a boon as the house was never just family. Beside elderly Miss Cox with her two rooms, we soon had evacuees: sometimes two aunts, one with young Peter, from Falmouth when the docks were being bombed or an odd soldier's wife down for their husbands week's leave who the vicar had persuaded Mother to squeeze in.

'Why doesn't he put them up in that b........... vicarage?' protested Dad, who rarely swore and objected to sleeping in the Morrison shelter in the kitchen. Baby sister followed us older ones around in our war games calling out, 'Joycee too'.

(RCM)

CHAPEL TEAS

These are held with great enjoyment and follow a time-honoured pattern. Long tables are made up of trestles and planks to go the whole length of the Sunday school. The tables are covered with starched white damask tablecloths and laid with white bone china, bordered in silver or gold leaf with the chapel's name proudly marked. Large plates laden with splits, buttered or spread with jam and clotted cream, white and saffron cake, iced fancies (bought from Wearne's of Helston) and slab (fruit cake) are put out together with vases of flowers here and there. At both ends of each table, the young ladies pour the tea and wait on everyone, bringing the cups of tea down the table and making sure they were refilled as soon as they emptied.

What a thrill it was to reach the age to be allowed to help. In the kitchen older ladies keep stocks up and the water boiling. Without being told, you knew that manners demanded you should start with a buttered split and that though you could eat as much as you liked of the cake, it would be greedy to eat more than one 'fancy'. Tea would be as most Cornish like it, very hot and strong with little milk.

After tea, while the ladies washed up, the men dismantled the tables and games were played: nursery rhymes, spinning the plate, stations, passing the parcel. Sometimes we would ask for postman's knock but the elders knew better and it was banned. Old photographs of chapel teas show the tables laid out of doors with no cover, but later a large marquee was hired.

FAITH TEA

Faith tea is similar to chapel tea but food is not bought. Each family brings a plateful of home cooking and it is surprising that the right proportion of savouries and cakes turn up, seemingly with no consultation.

Jam Paste (pasty pastry with jam)
sometimes called Windy Pasty

Roll out the pastry into a round. Spread a little butter or margarine on to one half. Fold over the other half. Do not egg wash. Bake in a hot oven for 15 minutes or so. Split open when cool. Spread each half with jam and clotted cream if liked.

Date Pasty (mock flaky pastry)

Place the dates in a bowl. Pour on boiling water and drain immediately. Roll out the pastry into a round or square. Cover one half with dates. Fold over the other half of the roll lightly with the rolling pin. Egg wash and bake in a moderate to hot oven, about 375°F/190°C/gas mark 5. Slices of cooking apples may be added to the dates. Alternatively an Eccles cake mixture can be used – 25g/1oz butter, 50g/2oz brown sugar, 20g/¾oz currants with a little peel, a dash of cinnamon.

Milk Splits

450g/1lb strong white flour
25g/1oz yeast and 1tsp sugar mixed together in a cup
50g/2oz lard
½ teaspoon salt
300ml/½pt milk, or milk and water

Mix the yeast and sugar into the tepid or cold liquid. Place the flour in a bowl, mix in the salt and rub in the fat. Pour in the liquid and knead well. Cover the mixture with a cloth and leave to prove. When doubled in size, cut into about ten 'splits' by moulding the pieces into balls, placing them on a greased tray quite close together and flattening the top lightly with the hand. Prove again. When the splits have doubled in size again, bake in a hot oven 400–425°F/200C–220°C/gas mark 6 for about 15 minutes. They are cooked when the bottoms are light brown.

42

When cool, cut the splits in half sideways; spread each half with strawberry, blackberry or blackcurrant jam and put a large dollop of clotted cream on top. 'Cornish cream teas' are a popular commercial treat, but scones (foreign and easier to make) have crept in instead of proper splits.

Yeast Cake

(Mrs June Hosking, Chyvarloe Farm, Gunwalloe)
1½kg/3lb strong flour and a pinch of salt
450g/1lb sultanas and, if you like, about 25g peel
40g/1½oz yeast
225g/8oz Trex
275g/10oz margarine
175g/6oz sugar
3 eggs
approx 560ml/1pt of milk to mix

Whisk the yeast into a little milk. Place the flour and salt in a bowl. Rub the fats into the flour; add sugar and fruit. Pour in the yeast liquid, the eggs and the remainder of the milk and stir with a knife to mix, then knead well. Cover the dough with a cloth and leave to prove. When doubled in size, knead again. Divide and mould into cakes, putting the dough into well greased tins. When it has risen again, place the cakes in an oven at 300°F/150°C/gas mark 2 and bake for one hour. Turn the cakes out onto a wire tray.

Note when using an electric mixer for yeast cakes, make the dough up and knead well before adding the fruit by hand. Fruit, especially currants, can discolour the dough when mixed in a machine.

Yeast Buns

450g/1lb strong white flour and a pinch of salt
50g/2oz margarine (or butter)
50g/2oz sugar
50g/2oz lard
175g/6oz sultanas
a little peel (optional)
25g/1oz yeast
1 egg (optional)

1 large cup milk (about 250ml/½pt) to mix
This recipe makes 16–20 buns.

Whisk the yeast into tepid or cold milk. Warm the flour if possible (not vital) and add the salt. Rub in the fats. Add the sugar and fruit, and mix in. Pour in the liquid and mix with a knife till all the liquid is absorbed. Finish by hand and knead well. Put the dough in a greased polythene bag or leave in a bowl and cover with a cloth to prove. When it has doubled in size, knead again lightly. Divide into 16 to 20 buns and place on a lightly greased baking tray. When the buns have doubled in size, bake in the oven at 400F/200°C/gas mark 6 for about 15 minutes. They are cooked when brown on the bottom. Bun dough should be of a softer consistency than cake mixture.

This week (May 2005) we had our opening faith tea in the bowling club at Helston and Joe (my husband) raved over this sponge sandwich. Mrs Hosken said I could use it in the book; she had learnt it from her mother. I've since baked it at home with great success. It's never too late to try a new recipe!

Fatless Sponge

(Mrs Joan Hosken, Tregowis, St Keverne)

Separate whites from yolks of three large (or 4 small) eggs. Beat whites till stiff as for meringues. Beat yolks and add to whites. Fold in ¾ teacup of caster sugar. Fold in one cup of self raising flour. Divide mixture between two greased sponge tins. Bake in moderate oven 375F/190°C/gas mark 5 for 15 minutes.

When I was a little 'maid' I was often puzzled by the expression, ''ee or she's as soft as Bunda'. Who was Bunda? I thought it must be a nickname; most men in fishing villages are known only by a nickname. I was grown up before I realised that 'Bunda' was bun dough. 'Like lance in jail' meaning extremely untidy was another phrase I never understood until years later. Launceston Jail must have been infamous for its reputation to spread so far – from the very edge of the county. In those days north of Truro was practically up-country.

SAFFRON

Saffron is the stamens of a certain type of crocus and nowadays it is imported mostly from Spain, although it is said that until the eighteenth century it was grown at Saffron Walden in Essex. Weight for weight it is more expensive than gold. 'As dear as saffron' is a very common Cornish expression. When I was sent sixty years ago for a shilling's worth, the grocer weighed a measure on special scales. In those days that amount of saffron coloured and flavoured 1.5kg/3lb of flour to a glorious yellow. Ten grains of saffron now costs nearly £2 and scarcely colours the same quantity darker than a primrose.

Saffron should be prepared the day before you need it. Place the strands in a cup. Pour boiling water on, and quarter fill the cup. Cover and leave in a safe place till use.

I lived in Stithians for a while and my neighbour, an elderly lady, Mrs Bath, prepared her saffron in a different way from any I had seen. She put her saffron between greaseproof paper and very carefully dried the strands. Then she rolled her rolling pin over the paper: this reduced the contents to powder. She said she got more flavour and colour from her saffron. I tried it once or twice, but I scorched the saffron and it was ruined, so I stick to soaking the strands, which I prefer to see in cakes.

Saffron Buns

450g /1lb strong white flour and a pinch of salt
225g/8oz cleaned currants
25g/1oz sultanas
50g/2oz sugar
50g/2oz butter
50g/2oz lard
25g/1oz fresh yeast
250ml/10fl oz (approx) tepid milk or milk and water to mix
peel, to taste
10 grains saffron (prepared the night before)

Whisk the yeast into the milk. Place the flour in a bowl with the salt and rub in the fats. Add the sugar and fruit, and stir in. Pour in the saffron first and rinse out the cup with the milk and yeast liquid. Mix the ingredients with a knife and then knead well. Put the dough aside in a bowl covered with a cloth to prove. When the dough has doubled in size, knead and divide into about 20 buns by shaping into balls and placing them on a greased baking tray. Flatten the tops of the buns with the hand and leave to prove, covering with a cloth. When the dough has doubled in size, bake at 400°F/200°C/gas mark 6 for about 15–20 minutes. They are cooked when brown on the bottom. An egg can be added to this recipe, adjusting the liquid if necessary.

Saffron Cake

(Mrs Lilian Stephen, Helston)
1kg/2lb 4oz strong white flour
175g/6oz butter
275g/10oz sugar
40g/1½oz yeast
200g/7oz lard
325g/11oz currants
100g/4oz sultanas
25g/1oz peel
1 egg (optional)
1 packet saffron 10 grains
400ml/¾pt milk and water

Steep the saffron overnight. Put the yeast into a teaspoonful of sugar and stir. Put the flour and salt in a bowl; rub in the fats. Add the sugar and stir in the fruit. Pour in the saffron and rinse out the cup with the milk; add the yeast liquid. Break the egg into the mixture, and mix with a knife till all the moisture is absorbed. Knead well. Cover the bowl with acloth. When it has doubled in size, knead lightly again. Cut the dough and place into well greased tins, three quarter filling them. Prove again. When the dough has risen a little way over the top of the tin, bake at 325°F/170°C/gas mark 3) for about an hour. When cooked, turn out at once onto a wire tray.

Not long ago I was reminiscing with Uncle Charlie. As children, his daughter and I were sent down to the quay with his 'croust' – a pint of hot strong tea in an enamel can with a cup hooked on the top and a couple of pieces of cake. It was almost always saffron and I commented to him that it was an expensive cake to be made so often and for croust! 'Well, my dear,' he said, 'I was earning really good money at that time, £7 or £8 a week.' It certainly was, but he earned it. His eyes used to be two rounds in a black face except where sweat ran down in trickles. He worked on the coal boats, helping unload tons of coal into the yards nearby. Everywhere along the harbour was covered in thick black coal dust.

Aunt Hartie, his wife, made a good saffron cake. She did something mother never did: she would cut across the dough with a big cross before proving. As the dough 'plumbed', the cross would get larger and larger. It served no purpose, but I have heard since that many housewives do this, probably unaware of the origin, making a sign of the cross to keep evil away. Mother only cut a cross on her Easter Friday saffron buns, made in place of hot cross buns.

One Christmas, Aunt Violet's saffron cake was a disaster. It didn't rise and the cake was heavy. There was a great discussion and some concern about this. In the end it was agreed among the aunts and Mother that it was too rich, too much goodness. I can remember visiting the house with Gran the day the cake was made and Aunt Violet taking down the bowl from the rack of the slab and anxiously examining the golden mound that was refusing to budge. Looking back, I don't think it was too much goodness that did the damage. Aunt Violet liked a good fire. The grate doors were often open, showing bright red embers through the iron bars. A wisp of steam always curled from a large black kettle on the range. When you had a cup of tea or cocoa you had to sip carefully lest you burnt your lip: the whole room was warm and cosy. I think the yeast was overcome by heat and expired. It is better to put a rich yeast mixture in the fridge overnight than near heat, though I do put the second proving near gentle warmth or on a sunny window ledge, so long as it's clear of any draught.

FEAST DAYS

Large saffron buns are the 'feast' bun of Cornwall. The bun, shrunk now from 30 to 15cm/12 to 6 in in diameter, is called a 'Tea Treat Bun'. Porthleven's feast day is 29 June, St Peter's Day.

Peverell Road, the fishermen's chapel celebrated on 30th 'Our Day'; Fore Street, the newer beautifully fronted church, 'Their Day'. This great feast St Peterstide recently has been held on the Saturday nearest these dates, both chapels joining with the Anglican church to make it one special day. The members set off from one of the places of worship at 2.30 pm to walk about two miles around the 'town' led by two bands and the churches' banners, to the recreation field, where every child of the Sunday schools was handed their bun. Gallons of free scalding tea was ready for anyone, prepared in the football team's changing hut.

Years ago a small team of men prepared tea in the field – the Tea Treat was then held in Kitto's net drying field. The area would be roped off from excited children, who seemed to be drawn like magnets to the scorching fire. It was hot work on a June day fetching water and making tea ready on time for hundreds of people, while the procession made its way round the village.

The route has changed little to this day – by Thomas Street, through The Unity, and wound up the Terrace, where a pause was made by the War Memorial to lay a wreath, pray and sing a hymn. Here the procession changed around, the first half letting the rest go forward to lead for the rest of the way, on down around the institute, along the harbour, the band striking up 'Onward Christian Soldiers' as it crossed the Square to Breagside. Here many little ones 'fell out' for a rest while the older scholars walked the final length past the Ship Inn up and down Breagside, rejoining the others to enter the field under the banners.

After a very brief prayer and doxology,

Be present at our table, Lord.
Be here and everywhere adored.

St Peterstide. I'm second from the right in the front, aged about 9, 1937. This is a family gathering with grandparents Gilbert in the centre (HM)

Each creature bless and grant that we
May feast in Paradise with Thee.

the children with their buns joined their families for a picnic tea. Everyone produced their own cups and the men brought round long jugs of tea, after which sports were held and the bands took their turn to play.

Nearby, in the old Withy Fields, a small fair catered mainly for the little ones. The fair families were old friends and my father could remember the names of the boys he played with when he was a lad, sons of Brewers and Jones. In earlier days the fair grouped around the harbour and it was an extra thrill to swing out in the swing boats over the edge of the harbour wall.

The thrill of this day was greater than any other holiday, more important than Christmas, Easter or birthdays. Relations from near and far came 'home' for the day and bunting hung from window to window outside the houses. White socks, plimsolls and new clothes had been waiting for weeks to be worn and the weather was discussed endlessly. Would it keep up if good, or clear if poor?

The atmosphere in the Sunday school, where for the last month we had been reluctantly drilled and taught our lines for Anniversary under the eagle eye of 'Popsie', was electric. By the time the procession set off, we were nearly worn out with excitement and running around – up one set of stairs, tip-toeing across the gallery, and down the other. The men, busy unfurling the large flags and beautiful blue and gold banner, for once turned a blind eye to our unholy behaviour. Outside, the bandsmen would be gathering, smart in their uniforms, chatting and smoking a last cigarette before the long walk.

All Cornish villages have their Feast Day, but only a few now march through the streets. The 'days', a whisper of our Celtic past, stretch all through the year according to whichever saint is remembered. It meant a day off from school, and was a nuisance for the County Education Office.

Popsie was our Sunday School teacher, a young widow who trained us for concerts. She was very strict and painstaking and we had to get word perfect, especially for anniversary when the men would build a platform underneath the pulpit in chapel. We were all crowded in on it, mostly girls dressed in pastel colours and black patent shoes. Mother sent me off once in a mulberry red dress and I stuck out like a sore thumb. Aunt Hartie said in a sad voice 'Poor Ida, she doesn't know any better'. Royal Ascot had nothing on Porthleven's Sunday clothes' parade.

The Christmas concert was fun. This was held in the Sunday School and we had the excitement of dressing up. I never see tinsel without remembering the crowded little vestry. There were always last minute repairs , the bigger girls hovering over us needle and cotton in hand to secure the shimmering stuff to our crepe paper dresses.

Popsie earned a meagre living giving piano lessons. She lived in Bay View Terrace, the row of graceful Victorian houses built in a gentle arc towards the town clock. They stand back from a high wall, which drops to the harbour road, and you get to them up stone steps and a right of way along the bottom of their little steep gardens. A stone's throw away is Salt Cellar Hill where the old men sat. We children played marbles aware of their quiet chatter. Weather was always discussed and tales retold.

My favourite tale is of two unmarried brothers, Charlie Oss and Buller who lived up-'n-town. Both were tall and thin and I never saw them smile. They were champion wreckers, always beachcombing the beach a mere 60 yards from their home. Their garden was chock-a-block with cuttle fish, wood, glass balls, and everything that had 'soo'd up'. They did odd jobs and one day were moving a piano for someone at Cliff Road. It was strapped onto a fisherman's flat barrow, usually used for carrying nets.

'Wheer you goin' with that there piano?' asked a passer-by. 'We'er goin down Popsie's for a piano lesson' Buller replied. This may not seem all that funny but to a local the mind takes over. They are already on a slope. Do they go bumping round the town clock's rough road, where they could lose control and land in the harbour, or would they squeeze through the narrow alley to Army Hill which is a steep path straight down to the pier, or could they manage the sharp right hand turn to go down steps to Bay View Terrace?

Of course, someone once got Popsie's piano into her house. It must be some job moving house or arranging a funeral, but I've never been around to see such a sight. It is a lovely place to live, but winter gales can be terrifying and at spring tides you could be trapped in your house for hours.

Mr Tregembo with his coal cart, where Charlie Oss and Buller were moving someone's piano 'strapped on a fisherman's flat barrow' (RCM)

51

Large saffron buns are the 'feast' buns of Cornwall. These buns are usually made with yeast but St Keverne has a different recipe.

St Keverne Feast Bun

(Mrs Mavis Sobey of St Keverne)
10 grains saffron prepared overnight
225g/8oz plain flour and a pinch of salt
225g/8oz self-raising flour
200g/7oz caster sugar
250g/9oz butter
175g/6oz dried fruit
milk and water to mix
egg and syrup for glaze

Rub the fat into the flour and salt. Add the dry ingredients and mix with the saffron and milk to form a dough that's a little softer than a pastry mixture. Roll out a little thinner than for scones. Cut out rounds and glaze with a mixture of egg and syrup. Mark a cross on the top of each bun with the back of a knife. Bake at 400°F/200°C/gas mark 6 for 15–20 minutes.

I was given this recipe by Mrs Mavis Sobey and would be interested to know if it is made in any other area. It is new to me and interesting, as it is a sort of saffroned 'heavy cake'. Mrs Sobey reduces the saffron to powder when she makes these buns.

Seed Cake

This cake was made very often by my mother and Gran Bray. It is about the only thing I cannot eat: I'd sooner eat snails.

My mother would make up her yeast cake mix without the fruit and divide a piece off for her 'seedy cake', adding about two tablespoons to a 1kg/2lb tin. Granny Bray, who never cooked with yeast, made a cake with a rubbing in method, which would have been 225g/8oz self raising flour. 85–115g/3–4oz butter, 85–115g/3–4oz sugar, 1 egg and a good tablespoon of caraway seeds mixed with milk or sour cream to a little softer consistency than rock buns. Put into a 20cm/8in cake tin and bake at 330°F/180°C/gas mark 4 for about an hour.

Heavy Cake

Heavy cake was, and is, a good standby. It is eggless and easily made. Farmers' wives made 'sheaves' full to be taken out in wicker flaskets for croust in the fields at harvest time, fresh and hot, with welcome cups of tea, it is surprisingly delicious. There are a great many recipes for heavy cake – here are two:–

Heavy Cake Made up Light

450g/1lb self raising flour
100g/4oz lard
125g/4½oz butter or margarine
100g/4oz sugar
300ml/ milk to mix
egg (optional)
a little peel (optional)
a good pinch of salt
175g/6oz currants and sultanas mixed

Rub the fats into the flour. Add the sugar, fruit, salt and milk, mixing with a knife till it becomes a dough. Place on a floured board and roll out 2cm/¾in thick. Score the top lightly. Brush with milk, water or egg. Place on a flat baking tray: cook for 20 minutes at 400°F/200°C/gas mark 6. Cut into good size squares.

An expert on Cornish cooking has told me that heavy cake should be 'shaley' on the top and have a 'heavy' line through the middle, and this might apply to the following recipe, though I have cheated a bit by using a little raising powder.

Proper Heavy Cake

225g/8oz mixed fruit (three quarters currants, the rest sultanas)
100g/4oz margarine
75g/3oz butter
400g/14oz plain flour
50g/2oz self-raising flour
a little peel (optional)
125g/4½oz lard
75g/3oz sugar
¼ teaspoon salt
300ml/½pt milk

Place the flour in a bowl. Rub in the lard and margarine lightly; add the sugar; salt and fruit. Mix with the milk. Roll out the mixture on a floured board. Dab butter on two-thirds of the surface; fold the unbuttered side over and fold again. Rest for 30 minutes. Roll out cake 2cm/¾in thick into a large round or square. Mark the top with the back of a knife with a net-like pattern and brush with milk. Cook at 375°F/190°C/gas mark 5 for about 20 minutes.

Some say heavy cake got its name from 'Hevva!', the cry the huer (the look-out on the cliffs) would shout when tell-tale signs of a shoal of fish appeared. It was the signal for the seiners to put to sea. Heavy cake is very popular in all the West Cornwall fishing ports and is never baked without the netlike pattern on top.

Douglas Bader of wartime fame spent his honeymoon in Porthleven on the recommendation of his flying friend Guy Gibson who led the Dambuster raid and whose mother came from an old established village family. Mr Bader didn't appreciate Porthleven, I think he found it all too quiet, an unsophisticated working community. He said the gulls wouldn't even eat the rock cakes they had been given to eat with a packed lunch. When I told a friend this wondering where he had stayed, she roared with laughter. 'They stayed with us' she said. This was at John Eddy Matthews' Atlantic Hotel, now a licensed premises. She added that her father, a strict non drinker, would turn in his grave if he knew.

I wonder if it was heavy cake that Mr Bader threw to the gulls. I can't believe that they refused it, gulls never refuse anything. In those days visitors paid £2 ten shillings a week full board. This was for breakfast, lunch, tea and evening dinner. Scarcely anyone had a car, so people walked a lot and usually ate a lot also. Mother used to get quite cross when people came all the way up from the beach for tea. I think they couldn't resist her lovely splits, jam and clotted cream filled buns dusted with icing sugar.

Sweet Buns
175g/6oz self-raising flour
125g/4½oz margarine
125g/4½oz caster sugar
50g/2oz mixed fruit
2 eggs

Cream the margarine and sugar till white and fluffy. Add the eggs; stir in the flour, mix well and add fruit gently. Spoon into greased bun tins or paper cases and bake in an oven at 350°– 400°F/180°–200°C/gas mark 4–6 for 10 to 15 minutes.

Congress Tarts

(Mrs Dale, Chyvarloe)
shortcrust pastry or flaky if preferred
125g/4½oz ground almonds
jam
125g/4½oz icing sugar
125g/4½oz caster sugar
75g/3oz ground rice
1 large egg
1 egg white

Prepare an almond filling by sieving the sugars, ground almonds and rice, and mixing with the egg. Line bun tins with pastry and put some jam in the centre. Fill the case with a good teaspoon of the almond filling. Put a cross of pastry on the top and bake in the middle of the oven at 350°F/180°C/gas mark 4 for about half an hour. When they are pale brown on the bottom, they should be cooked.

Coconut Haystacks

small tin condensed milk
225g/8oz desiccated coconut
Mix together; to make haystacks, press even amounts of the mixture into a lightly greased egg cup. Shake out carefully onto greased baking sheet. Bake at 300–350°F/150°–180°C/gas mark 2–4 for about 15 minutes until very light brown.

Ginger Biscuits

100g/4oz self-raising flour
50g/2oz lard and butter mixed
2 tablespoons golden syrup
1 level teaspoon cinnamon
2 level teaspoons ginger
1 level dessertspoon granulated sugar
½ teaspoon bicarbonate of soda

Sieve the dry ingredients. Melt the fats and syrup, then cool them and mix all the ingredients together. Break off pieces about the size of a walnut and place, well spaced, on a lightly greased baking tray. Bake for 15 minutes at 375°F/190°C/gas mark 5.

This is not the old 'Fairing' recipe, which is treasured secret in some families and made a fortune for one.

Chocolate Cake

2 level teaspoons coffee powder (optional)
1 level teaspoon bicarbonate of soda
200g/7oz plain flour
4 level tablespoons cocoa
2–3 teaspoons lemon juice
180ml/6fl oz milk
175g/6 oz caster sugar
125g/4½oz butter
2 eggs, beaten

Sieve the cocoa, flour and coffee powder together. Beat the butter and sugar together till light. Beat in the eggs. Put the lemon juice into the milk, then add the bicarbonate of soda. Fold in the flour mixture together with the milk mixture. Put into a greased bread tin the size for a large loaf if you are making a cake; or in a Swiss roll tin for a gateau. For a cake, bake at 375°F/190°C/gas mark 5 for 40–60 minutes, testing with a skewer at 40 minutes. A gateau will need less time. When cool, ice the cake with your favourite icing, or try 100g/4oz plain chocolate. 1 tablespoonful of rum and 25g/1oz butter, gently melted together. This cake improves with keeping.

For a gateau, turn out the chocolate sponge on to a wire tray. When almost cool, coat the top with 225g/8oz plain chocolate melted with 2 tablespoons of milk. When cold and firm, turn the cake over: spread the surface with some jam or raspberries, and then whipped double cream. Grate some chocolate on top.

Mrs Champion's Christmas Cake

One Christmas we were staying at Gunwalloe and Mrs Champion invited us to tea. They had a lovely old farm kitchen and my brother and I were put to sit in the window seat, our feet barely touching the floor. On the table was the most magnificent fruit cake I had ever seen. It was plainly iced with something red stuck in the middle, but between the icing and the cake was a good 5cm/2in of marzipan.

By now I should think that anyone reading this will have realised that I was a child who loved her tummy. I cannot remember what else we had for tea that day. I know the table groaned, and that that cake has stayed in my mind ever since.

Here are a few more recipes from the booklet from 1939, including Mrs Champion's cake.

Holly and Robin Cake

(Mrs E Champion, Chinalls, Gunwalloe)
450g/1lb self-raising flour
a good pinch of salt
340g/12oz butter
340g/12oz caster sugar
450g/1lb sultanas
450g/1lb currants
115g/4oz candied peel
50g/2oz sweet almonds
115g/4oz glace cherries
1 tablespoon treacle
5 fresh eggs
1 tablespoon brandy
1 teaspoon mixed spice
a pinch of nutmeg
grated rind of half a lemon
juice of a small lemon
1 dessertspoon caramel if a very dark cake is required

Prepare the fruit, shred peel; cut cherries into quarters. Blanch, skin and chop the almonds, grate the lemon rind and add to the sieved flour with the salt and spices. Cream the butter and sugar, beating well together until thoroughly blended. Beat in each egg separately with a tablespoon of flour. Stir in the dry ingredients, then the lemon juice, adding a little milk if necessary. Stir in the treacle, sufficient caramel to darken the cake, then the brandy. Pour the mixture into a prepared tin and scoop the centre of the cake towards the edges, making these higher so that the cake will bake level. Bake in a moderate oven at 350°F/180°C/gas mark 4 for 1½ hours, then reduce to 275°F/140°C/gas mark 1. Allow from four to five hours. When cold, wrap the cake in greaseproof paper and store for one month. Decorate with almond paste and icing.

Genoa Cake

(Mrs M Freeman, Tregadjack, Mawgan)
275g/10oz plain flour sieved with 1 tsp baking powder
225g/8oz caster sugar
450g/1lb currants
115g/4oz almonds
225g/8oz butter
115g/4oz sultanas
275g/10oz candied peel
grated rind of lemon
3 eggs

Blanch the almonds and cut them in pieces. Wash the currants and clean the sultanas, beat the sugar and butter until light and creamy, add the flour, beat in the eggs and add the fruit and stir well. Paper a shallow tin, pour in mixture and bake in a moderate oven 350°F/180°C/gas mark 4 from 1 to 1½ hours. When cooked, brush top with white of egg and strew with chopped almonds.

Note: This would be an excellent traybake. Omit nuts; when cooked and cooled, spread with jam and cover with a thin layer of marzipan and then lemon icing.

Home Made Toffee

(Miss Susan Joan Howe, Gunwalloe)
115g/4oz butter
340g/12oz brown sugar
175g/12oz syrup
1 teaspoon lemon juice
1 teaspoon water

Melt the ingredients, bring to the boil slowly and continue boiling for 15 minutes – stirring all the time. Test whether sufficiently cooked by placing a teaspoonful of toffee in a cup of cold water, when it should set quite firmly. Now pour molten toffee into buttered tins and, when cold, break into pieces.

Grandmother's Cake

(Mrs Stewart Lugg, Toll, Gunwalloe)
1 rounded teaspoon bicarbonate of soda
225g/1 cup brown sugar
400g/3½ cups flour
1 level tablespoon cinnamon
½pt/1 cup thick sour cream
450g/1lb stoned raisins
½ cup treacle

Measure with a 280ml/½pt teacup. Pour the slightly warmed treacle into the mixing bowl, add the soda dissolved in a little warm water, then work in the flour, sugar and cream. Beat well, add cinnamon and raisins. Bake in a moderate oven for one hour.

Walnut Gingerbread

(Mrs Owen Lugg, Gunwalloe)
3 cups flour
½ cup milk
1 teaspoon bircarb.
½ cup butter
1 cup Lyle's golden syrup
½ cup sugar
1 teaspoon ground ginger
1 cup chopped walnuts
pinch of salt

Beat the butter and sugar, Stir in the ginger and syrup. Dissolve the bicarbonate of soda in milk, add to the mixture with sifted flour, salt and walnuts. Pour into a greased shallow tin – a roasting dish. Bake in a moderate oven for one hour.

St Peterstide Procession on Breageside 24 June 1925 (RCM)

FRUIT

Fruit was usually bought for special occasions. An orange each in the Christmas stocking was an annual treat. Quite often, Gran Gilbert, who liked oranges, would buy a couple of Jaffas, large and juicy. Granddad, who had been to Africa steamboating and was stranded there for three years during the Boer War, insisted the orange be peeled the right way that so the pith came off cleanly. The orange would then be divided into 'pasties' and shared around. Gran saved the peel to simmer gently with sugar and a little water till it candied, and carefully smoothed out the large coloured square of tissue paper that the orange had been wrapped in, for her use and mine! Lemons too were beautifully wrapped. Lemons were for pancakes and drinks, cold in summer and hot in winter.

Granddad was very young when he went round the world. He brought back stalks of bananas and exciting bits and pieces like calabashes for his young family. (They had eight children, two died in infancy). Granddad Gilbert always left a little food on his plate to feed the gulls. One gull in particular alighted on the shed opposite whenever Pap put his head out of the door. As soon as he heard the scrape of a knife against the plate, the gull would lift its head and call. I thought how silly it was, as he could have had all the food to himself.

Grapes were bought, as they are now, for anyone ill. Strawberries were a treat at St Peterstide. We picked loads of blackberries in season and there were windfalls from the apple trees at *Content*, where Uncle Fred also had many gooseberry, blackcurrant, raspberry and loganberry bushes. Rhubarb was grown by Uncle George, who had an allotment, and by Uncle Charlie, both keen gardeners.

Dried fruits, apricots figs and especially prunes were very popular. Tinned pears or peaches might be bought for a special treat for Sunday teatime, but usually it was jelly and custard or blancmange and prunes, 'which are good for you'.

SUPPER OR LATE TEA

For this something savoury was preferred. Salted cod or fresh fish, fried or 'scrowled' over the fire, tripe and onions, hogs pudding from the butcher or liver fried with onions, ham from a knuckle, marinated pilchards or fish and chips from Tregembo's where 'Harry' would cook pollack specially for Gran. A piece of leftover pasty would fill a gap or tasty sausages from James' shop in Helston. Sausages and 'scrowls' (pork scratchings) could be bought too, from Mrs Eddy's house in the little island beside Fore Street Chapel.

I can just remember visiting Mrs Eddy with Gran: the long crowded old room was darkened by masses of leaves and bushes outside her far window and beside Mrs Eddy was her parrot, of whom I was terrified. Mrs Eddy was a character and surely harmless, hut I hung on to Gran's long black skirts – petrified.

Granddad Gilbert, in the middle, on the quay at Porthleven about 1946 (HM)

Hog's pudding is a kind of 'white' black pudding, and its recipes are closely guarded, but this sausage recipe is very good.

Sausages

450g/1lb bread (stale)
1½kg/3lb lean pork
450g/1lb fat pork (not flare)
25g/1oz salt
1½ level tsp ground mace
½ level tsp ground ginger
¼ level tsp ground or chopped sage
some flour
900ml/1½pt cold water

Soak the bread in 900ml/1½pt cold water. Put the pork through a coarse mincer. Add salt and seasonings. Mix well. Squeeze water from the bread and mix it with the meat mixture. Replace the mincer with a small cutter and put the mixture through again. Test for salt by frying a little sausage in a pan, adjusting seasoning if necessary. Shape into sausages with flour. Cook for 20 minutes or so.

Marinated Pilchards

Take a dozen or so pilchards. Gut, scrape off the scales and head and tail them but leave in the bones. Wash and lay them neatly close together in a pie dish, sprinkle with a few whole pickling spices, a little salt, pepper and sugar to taste, and cover with a mixture of three parts malt vinegar to one part water, laying bay leaves along the top. Cover with greaseproof paper and then with a piece of brown paper, tucking the paper around the dish edge to seal. Put into a hot oven till bubbling, then turn down the heat to 200°F/90°–100°C/the lowest gas mark you have.

Cook gently for at least 24 hours. Eat cold. Spiced vinegar may be used instead of malt vinegar and spices. The bones should be soft enough to eat.

DRINKS

There was tea to drink for the grown ups and cocoa for the children. Coffee was almost unknown except for Camp coffee with chicory.

Gran Gilbert made real lemonade. If she thought we needed 'building up' she would make an egg nog (egg whisked into hot milk with a little sugar and nutmeg added). There were also liver salts to clean out our systems. These salts were just like the commercial ones, but no one in the family can remember the recipe. There was no escape from Syrup of Figs, a weekly dose. Alcohol was rarely bought. Uncle George made gallons of non-alcoholic 'herby beer', which is very refreshing. Herby beer can be made by buying a bottle of herb beer mixture from a good chemist and following the instructions.

At *Content*, Aunt Hettie made blackberry wine. This was surprising as she was strictly tee-total. Aunt Hettie lived with her in-laws and I think she made wine after her father-in-law died. He was a dear old man, staunchly Methodist and a local preacher. It was a tied cottage, but once it had been a holding in its own right. The kitchen with its bare red flagged tiles worn with age reminded me of my favourite book, *Lorna Doone*. The room was large and looked sparsely furnished but it had a long wooden scrubbed table in front of the window, a big carver for Uncle Fred to sit in (after his father died), a large armchair, lots of small chairs and another table with plants on. A large china dresser stood against a wall which was partitioned off from a back room. Built into the old fireplace were cupboards each side of a Cornish range. Kindling wood was kept in these, whole long branches in one, the day's supply in the other. They were usually apple branches. The lichen fell off in great pieces and insects and gramma sows (woodlice) crawled everywhere. Aunt Hettie swept them up with a witch's broom. The fireplace extended through to the other side of the wall and there you could walk into an enormous chimney and look up at the sky.

About a hundred years ago the gardens around the house had been well laid out. A lemon tree leaned against the house and roses climbed around the corner and over the outside closet. All the way up to the orchard were hydrangea, rose and fruit bushes~ all tangled up. In front of the house a small lawn tried hard to survive. Here Aunt Hettie reared her baby chicks in coops where she could keep her eye on them and they had some protection from owls, foxes and buzzards. Beyond was another copse surrounded by tall trees. It was a wonderful secret place for us children. Pampas bushes and pittosporam towered over us and brambles held us captive. It was cool and dark, the foliage letting in little shafts of sunlight here and there. I was puzzled by the number of shiny brown bottles lying everywhere. When you trod on them they didn't break but sank into the soft mulch of pine needles, small branches and rotting leaves.

Years later Aunt Hettie told me that Uncle Fred used to bring home a couple of bottles of beer for his mother when he went to town on his motorbike. Mrs Reed smuggled them upstairs to drink and would not be seen bringing them down empty so she used to fling them from her bedroom window across the little grass patch, sometimes hitting the beautiful laburnum tree in the centre. Mrs Reed was born at Helford, and was, I suspect, Church of England. It must have been hard for two strong minded women isolated together with two rather dour men, but for all of us who visited, it was heaven.

There were several *Contents*. *Content* proper, then *Higher, Lower and Little*. All but *Little* were swept away to make room for Culdrose Naval Air Station. *Little Content* with its cows and view of Loe Pool remains mere yards from the main entrance, but the same road leads down to Tangies, Chyvarloe and Gunwalloe, a delight all year with gorse, may, primroses, bluebells and cow parsley in spring and a favourite place in autumn for blackberrying as it has been in the past for generations of Helstonians.

There was and probably still is a great divide between chapel and church, but the fact is that before Wesley visited Cornwall there were several 'kiddlywinks' in every Cornish village, however small. Some of the old Cornish drinks sound lethal, but certainly warming. 'Samson' is cider and rum boiled together with honey. 'Chenagrum' is hot beer, rum, sliced lemon, nutmeg and sugar. 'Christmas drink' consists of two lumps of sugar, a wineglass of rum, lemon and hot water. 'Mahogany' is two parts gin to one part treacle. Cornish 'punch' can be made with half a bottle of cognac, a tumbler of lemon juice, 2–4 lb/1–2kg cane sugar; all put into a gallon container and filled up with boiling water.

Granddad Bray had a good supply of red wine. At some date in the thirties kegs of wine had washed in on the shore from Fishing Cove to Praa Sands. I have been told that they were pipes (over two metres tall) and that it was raw claret, not yet matured. This wine lasted years and a bottle at a time was kept in the little Bible cupboard beside the fireplace in Granddad's sitting room. Occasionally my brother and I would be allowed to have some. A quarter tumbler of red wine, a large spoonful of sugar, and the glass topped up with hot water. We didn't tell Gran at Porthleven.

One evening Father and Mother went from Porthleven to Gunwalloe to fetch some of the wine. It's a long walk across the cliffs, separated halfway by a good ten minutes' trudge on shingle – the Loe Bar. On the way back, after crossing the Bar, they sat, emptied their shoes of pebbles and rested a while. They were getting anxious about the time when they saw a man approaching, pushing his bike across the stretch towards them. It was now dusk and they stood up to make enquiries. Father was six feet tall; mother tall also, thin as a wraith. The two figures suddenly rising out of the ground in the gloom, bottles clinking in the frail they were carrying, was too much for the poor man. He turned tail, bike and all, and was swallowed up in the darkness. In vain father shouted to reassure him, 'It's only me, Percy Gilbert'. They never found out who he was. In those days the Loe Bar route from Gunwalloe or Mullion was a short cut, saving miles around Helston for people who lived at Breage and Ashton as well as Porthleven.

Porthleven had few 'gentry'. The squire, a couple of miles away in his manor at Penrose, was distant and his great authority did not affect the fishermen, who did not depend on his goodwill for work or housing. There was the vicar, 'well educated', liked and tolerated though Pap did not approve of him dressing in a 'frock'. The Methodist ministers were respected, but in their place. The chapels were firmly run by stewards. As for Doctor Elliston, his word was gospel and his advice is quoted still.

Doctor Elliston's wife was a genteel woman, very generous with her food. 'Doctor' liked a good table. They had one daughter, Hope. When the family had finished their dinner, the servants were welcome to cut as much meat off the joint as they wished for their own meal. This was unusual then, and would be more than generous today. Mother, Bella and Trissie tucked in, in true Cornish style.

Mrs Elliston also permitted mother to take home any poultry carcasses for Granny Gilbert. This was a great treat as the bones were quite well covered. Gran would pick off all the meat and make broth with the bones. Once when Gran Gilbert was ill, Mrs Elliston sent down a huge two pint moulded Russian cream. It sat on a plate on the washstand by Gran's bedside, firm as a rock with three clear layers. I know now that it must have had more gelatine in it than Mother's, whose Russian cream when turned out slowly subsided and was a lovely light texture. I know I eyed that Russian cream, but cannot remember eating any of it. Ill or not, Gran probably ate the lot.

Mother made ice-cream. Granddad Gilbert fetched dry ice from Pawlyn's to freeze the custard and we all helped with turning the handle of the wooden tub it was made in. At Christmas she made about a dozen cakes. Some were three colour sponges with soft butter fillings, others walnut, covered with American icing, which I have never mastered as well. There were saffron cakes and rich fruit ones which mother would struggle to ice. We are lucky today with ingredients all ready and easy to use.

Puddings and cakes took a day to prepare. Currants had to be thoroughly washed, spread out on paper and put in a rack overnight to dry. Raisins needed stoning, a lovely sticky job, and sultanas were put in a large sieve and two or three lots of flour shaken through them till the flour came out clean. Almonds were blanched and chopped, and the butter and sugar had a beat from two or three of us to get it soft and fluffy. When the cake was made, Mother would open the oven door and feel the heat before putting the cake in and wait anxiously till it was safely out of the oven without burning – there was no thermostat on a slab!

I think the hardest job of all was icing the cakes. Was all icing sugar as lumpy as Mum's? I can hear the crunch now as she rolled and rolled the lumps out. Then she shook the sugar through a fine sieve. She wrote 'Merry Christmas' beautifully on each cake, but sometimes a piece of sugar would stick in the nozzle and the whole lot would have to be put back in the bowl and the icing gun washed out in hot water.

Father would fuss at all this activity for neighbours and relations, but it made no difference: Christmas wouldn't have been the same without all that cooking.

Mother's nearest neighbours were Mr and Mrs Peter Williams whose house was built slightly lower than ours. Wooden steps placed against their wall saved walking down our path and up theirs. The Williams' kitchen was almost as familiar as our own. The room was rather dark because a glass-roofed outer room had been built on, but the light seemed to shine onto a picture of an old man kneeling on a form in a plain chapel. He was praying and it seemed to bless the kitchen table immediately below the picture. I thought the old man looked like Willie Allen who sat downstairs in the middle of the chapel. He sold fish all week, but on Sundays he looked different in his best suit; his bald head, hatless shone 'like a dollar'. We sat above in the gallery in our family seat and for the morning service we were free of grown-ups. My cousins André

Brooklyn, Peverell Terrace, Porthleven 1936 – my home with mother and the Gilbert grandparents and brother John (HM)

and Jack flicked rolled up sweet papers at Mr Allen's head. He never batted an eyelid even when they scored a direct hit. In the front seat of the gallery opposite, Margaret Jane Toy, father's cousin, frowned at all of us.

The slab in Mrs Williams' kitchen was in the far corner where Tiny the dog slept for most of the day in a chair beside it. A door with a tiny knob hid the narrow stairs which led to the back rooms where the three sons slept. Mr and Mrs Williams had a business at the foot of Salt Cellar Hill on the quay and Mother often lit their slab during the late afternoon. It was a cantankerous old thing and she sometimes doused it with paraffin to get it going. One day she poured a good drop over and when she threw in the lighted march there was an almighty bang and the dog was shot from one end of the room to the other.

Hugh, one of the boys, had left petrol in the can. After that the dog ran away whenever he saw mother coming.

I was envious of the boys. They wore huge aprons for their Sunday meals. This seemed a good idea to me: I had to change. As soon as I got in from chapel I had to go upstairs, take off my Sunday dress, put on another, then change again for Sunday school and go through the same performance later for tea. The truth is I could not be trusted with a piny; summer best was that awful crêpe-de-chine which was murder to wash.

Food has changed quite a bit everywhere during the past few decades. The farmers' wives no longer cook large joints of 'tag' or 'boxheater' for harvest dinners – combine harvesters have done away with the need for a dozen or so men working in the field shocking up the corn, or helping on threshing day with the old steam thresher, which went from farm to farm at the end of summer.

No one seems to have the time to spend in the kitchen, cooking the quantities our mothers and grandmothers did. We can only look back and marvel at their good tempers in the face of baking, washing and ironing all around the slab, and coping with its 'smeach' when it smoked. It had to be riddled, lit, tended, coached and cleaned every day till it shone black. There it was, the centre of our lives, brass handles shining, cooking dinners and baking in its oven. It kept the kettle hot and clothes on the boil: there was room to heat the iron, scald cream and dry off kindling wood, all on the surface. The rack provided the right warmth to raise the yeast and air clean clothes. New baby chicks could be nursed in the fender and wet shoes and boots dried overnight.

Will our children and grandchildren have the same regard for the electric or gas cooker; for fish fingers and baked beans; for Milky Bars instead of jam paste to fill up a gap on the way home from school?

Two world wars and time has changed the way everyone lives. The village has grown beyond belief. Cars have replaced walking and television the old intimacy of a chat. The need that every man had a nickname to distinguish them, has gone. Who now knows who is, or why 'Tommy Cuddle', 'Georgie Lad', 'Rasputin' or 'My wife, Miss Blewett', got their special names and nearly two hundred others, theirs?

I feel I was lucky. I lived half my childhood with Gran and Granddad. The village was a close-knit community and we knew everyone. It was full of aunts, uncles and cousins, and I traipsed around with Gran to them all, from Auntie Violet's cocoa to sweet buns from Auntie Annie, heavy cake at Aunt Hartie's. Wonderful holidays all months of the year at *Content*.

We lived and worked in an environment that had not changed for a long time. The legacy those days left is rich and I hope its values will not disappear completely.

The Lugg family at *Content*, harvesting with Uncle Fred on the rick. 1930s (HM)